VC
24

NW

WASHOE COUNTY LIBRARY

3 1235 03346 5696

D0765679

No Longer Property Of
Washoe County Library

SNAILOLOGY

SNAILOLOGY

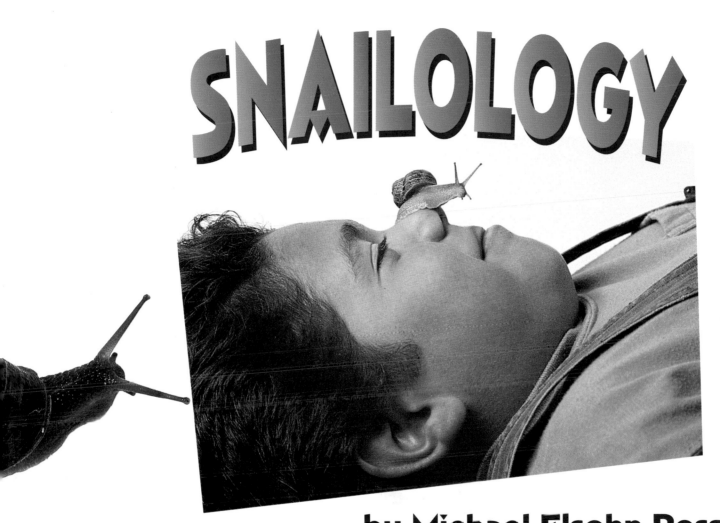

by Michael Elsohn Ross

photographs by Brian Grogan • illustrations by Darren Erickson

Carolrhoda Books, Inc. / Minneapolis

To Frances, who appreciates all creatures, no matter how odd.

Without the creativity and enthusiasm of the second- through sixth-grade students of El Portal Elementary and the support of their teachers, Carl Brownless and Phyllis Weber, this book would not have been possible. The author would also like to thank the students of Vista de Valle School in Claremont, California, and Tom Jones and his students at Alicia Reyes School in Merced, California, for their assistance.

Text copyright © 1996 by Michael Elsohn Ross
Photographs copyright © 1996 by Brian Grogan
Illustrations copyright © 1996 by Carolrhoda Books, Inc.

All rights reserved. International copyright secured. No part of this book may be reproduced, stored in a retrieval system, or transmitted in any form or by any means, electronic, mechanical, photocopying, recording, or otherwise, without the prior written permission of Carolrhoda Books, Inc., except for the inclusion of brief quotations in an acknowledged review.

Carolrhoda Books, Inc.
A Division of the Lerner Publishing Group
241 First Avenue North, Minneapolis, MN 55401

Website address: www.lernerbooks.com

LIBRARY OF CONGRESS CATALOGING-IN-PUBLICATIONS DATA

Ross, Michael Elsohn, 1952–
    Snailology / by Michael Elsohn Ross ; photographs by Brian Grogan ; illustrations by Darren Erickson.
        p.   cm. — (Backyard buddies)
    Includes index.
    Summary: Provides instructions for finding, collecting, and keeping snails and suggests how to delve into the secret lives of these shell dwellers.
    ISBN: 0-87614-894-1
    1. Snails — Juvenile literature. 2. Snails — Experiments — Juvenile literature. 3. Snails as pets — Juvenile literature. [1. Snails.] I. Grogan, Brian, 1951–   ill. II. Erickson, Darren, ill. III. Title. IV. Series: Ross, Michael Elsohn, 1952–   Backyard buddes.
    QL430.4.R67 1996
    594'.3 — dc20   95-30900

Manufactured in the United States of America
2 3 4 5 6 7 - JR - 04 03 02 01 00 99

Contents

Would you slide across the floor

and roam up a door?

Could you cruise on slime

and have a great time?

Could you follow the trail

of a slippery garden snail?

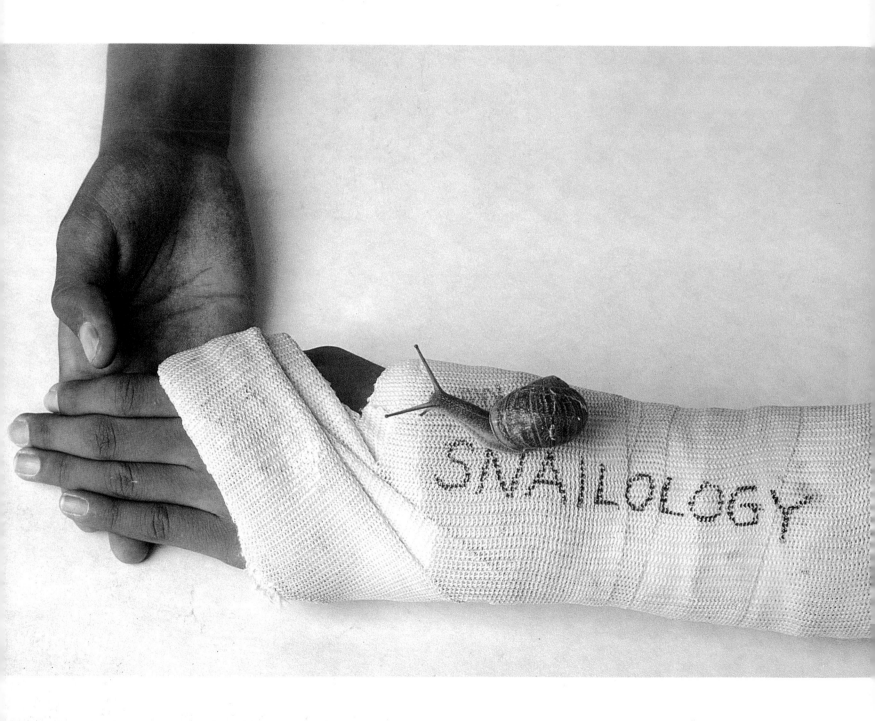

Meet the garden snail. You may know that it is slow, slimy, and shelled, but what else do you know? Have you ever picked one up and introduced yourself?

Welcome to Snailology

(fear of slime). Most kids, on the other hand, are secretly (or not) intrigued by spit, snot, and other gooey, gloopy stuff. Admit it. Haven't you ever played with your ice cream or concocted gloppy mixes in the kitchen? Haven't you been through phases when you played with spit or even snot? Perhaps it's part of what being a kid is all about.

Geologists study rocks, meteorologists try to unravel the weather, and snailologists get acquainted with slimy neighbors. To be a snailologist, all you need is a curiosity about the slow, shell-dwelling creatures we know as snails. Be a gentle explorer, and enjoy your journey to snail land.

Snails do not bite, sting, or scratch. Though they pose no danger, snails often strike panic into the hearts of normally courageous adults. This mysterious condition is the result of slimophobia

Since snails leave a trail, a little backyard slime tracking should help you find some. Examine the ground and vegetation for irregular, criss-crossing tracks that glitter in the sunlight. Feel the tracks. If they are still slimy, an active snail or slug is nearby. If they are dry, you probably have some resting ones in the vicinity. Poking about under rocks, leaves, and debris should reveal their hiding places.

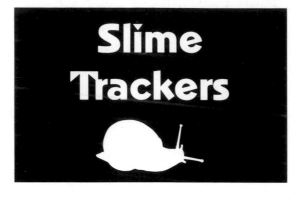

If you don't have any snails where you live, check with local gardeners. They'll know if any snails exist in their gardens and should be only too glad to let you collect them.

Place your snails in a container with a lid to keep them from escaping. Your guests will appreciate being kept in the shade, since direct sunlight can dry them up and kill them! Even though they are housed in a shell, they can still be hurt unless they are handled with care. Remember, to a snail, humans are giants. Be a gentle one.

Before you skip into the house with your new guests, picture how your parents will react. Will they climb upon the counter in fright, order you to return the snails to the wild, or snatch them for their new French recipe?

With some fast talk, you may be able to prepare them for your new visitors. "I was thinking about asking for a pit bull for my next birthday, but then I found these harmless, adorable creatures in our backyard. They don't run around, bark, or need canned food. You can keep them in a jar, and all they eat is leaves. Can they be houseguests for just a few days?"

Corralling wild horses is nothing compared to hosting snails. Snails can't gallop or jump fences, but they are pretty outstanding climbers. If you're not careful, your slimy friends may get loose and cause a minor panic in your household. Below are some tips to assist you in providing a safe and comfortable corral for your new friends.

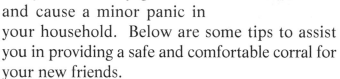

You will need:

✔ a plastic tub with a lid, or a dishpan with a board large enough to cover it
✔ soil
✔ lettuce or other green leaves
✔ paper, pen, tape

Be sure to get permission before you use kitchen stuff.

Snail Corral Construction

1. Sprinkle a 1-inch layer of moist soil on the bottom of the tub. The soil should feel damp, but not soggy. If you are using a dishpan, find a flat board or piece of wood for a lid. Make sure it fits tightly. Ask an adult to help you make holes in the lid or board for air.

2. Drop some lettuce in the corral. Outer lettuce leaves are tossed away by most grocery stores and are often available for free.

3. Gently place your snails on the lettuce and cover the corral.

4. Attach a sign that says who lives inside so no one will be surprised if they take a peek.

5. Keep the corral in a dark cupboard or closet and reward your snails by letting them rest. Hang up a "Do Not Disturb" sign and kiss them good night.

Once your corralled pals have had a chance to rest, satisfy your curiosity and take a peek. As you lift off their roof, imagine you are a giant keeping an eye on your new friends. Though most giants may consider little creatures boring, you know different. As you watch your snail guests, you realize how easy it will be to dispel the silly notion that giants lack respect for tiny folk. Take some time to sit and watch your small, slimy friends. Make a short list of all the strange actions of your guests and then display it for others to read.

Giant Caretaker

You need not pretend you are a giant anymore! In reality, you *are* a giant, and there are plenty of people who do not allow themselves to find fascination in little living creatures. If you make a real list and display it on the lid of the snail corral, perhaps you'll be able to challenge friends and family to make their own discoveries. After a few days of snail snooping, review the sightings. Do you notice any patterns of behavior? Do they always do the same thing? Do they act different at night? Do you think they are keeping notes on you?

Do you think your snails need a little exercise? Have you ever considered making a gym for snails? A large baking pan (used with the cook's permission) will keep the snails contained for a while. All you need to do is fill it with some entertaining equipment. Below are a few ideas to get you thinking, but no doubt you're already brewing up some plans of your own!

Snail Gymnasium

Let a snail loose in the gym. What does it do? Perhaps you can take some notes to add to your snail corral list. If you think your snail needs company, add a few more snails. What do you think will happen?

Would you like to become gym equipment? All you need to do is place a snail on your hand and sit still. Can it climb your arm? Does it tickle?

Be sure to return the snails to their corral after you are finished. Not only is a house a dangerous place for a wandering snail, but slime trails on the walls and ceiling could make it a dangerous place for you too!

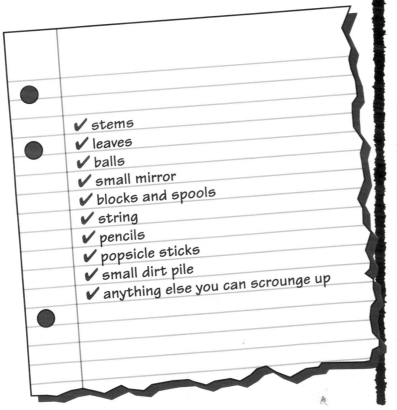

✔ stems
✔ leaves
✔ balls
✔ small mirror
✔ blocks and spools
✔ string
✔ pencils
✔ popsicle sticks
✔ small dirt pile
✔ anything else you can scrounge up

Are you aware? Would you notice if your dad got his nose pierced and his hair permed? Would you notice if your best friend grew six inches overnight? Do you notice small details? Whatever your answers, the Aware Dare is for you. If you are totally unaware, then this game will help you tune in to trivia. Being tuned in is very helpful when you are getting acquainted with new critters, such as snails. On the other hand, if you are totally aware, this game will provide yet another opportunity to display your amazing abilities. Though it can be played alone, the Aware Dare is more fun with two or more players.

You will need:

✔ one snail
✔ a magnifying lens
✔ a moist paper towel
✔ optional: pen or pencil and paper

How to Play

1. Decide on the order of play. *Optional:* pick one player to record what each of you notices.

2. Place the snail on the moist paper towel and then give it a good look.

3. Beginning with player number 1, take turns sharing observations. For example, you might say "It has a shell," or "It's not moving." Any detail is okay, but no repeats are allowed. However, more items can be added to a previous account. For example, though someone may have said, "It has a shell," another person can still say, "It has a brown shell."

4. Continue taking turns in the same order until only one player is able to make a new observation. The last person to share a snail detail is the champion observer.

If you were shopping for a bicycle, would you notice if it was missing standard equipment such as a pair of wheels, chain, kickstand, or handlebars? Of course! Did you ever wonder what standard equipment and features snails come with? The items listed below might prove helpful in checking out your snails.

Standard Equipment

Parts: How many different kinds of parts can you see? What do they look like? Are there nostrils, cheeks, or fingernails? Are the parts in different shapes? How many shapes can you see?

Speed: What kinds of speeds are the snails capable of? Set snails one at a time in the middle of a sheet of paper and then record the time it takes each one to cruise off. Do all of your snails move at the same speed? What's the record time?

Shell: With the ruler, you can determine what sizes snails come in. How big is the biggest? How small is the smallest? Are they the same color? Do they all have the same number of spirals?

Weight: How hefty can a snail get? Weigh your snails and keep track of their weight over a few weeks. By marking their shells with nontoxic, water-soluble colored markers (which won't harm the snails), you can identify each individual snail. Do you think they'll gain weight under your care?

You will need:

✔ a watch with a second hand
✔ a ruler
✔ a magnifying lens
✔ a pencil and paper
✔ one or more snails
✔ a blank sheet of paper
✔ a kitchen scale

Paintings of famous characters are on display in art museums all over the world. Unfortunately, few of these portraits' illustrious subjects were snails. Here's a chance to fix this unfair situation. Create your own famous snail art!

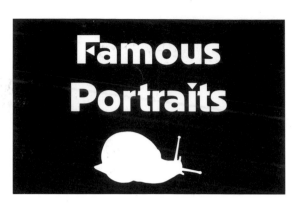

2. Warm Up Your Fingers: Each time your ant eyes reach a new part of the snail, make a quick sketch of it. This will loosen your hand and your mind. It will prepare you for the creation of a big picture.

3. Regard Your Curiosity: If questions such as "What is that thing called?" pop into your noggin, jot them down next to your drawings. Questions are well worth collecting.

4. Almost There . . . : Before starting your final portrait, you may find it helpful to polish off a few rough sketches of the basic shape and outline of your model.

5. Work Big: It's easier to include small details when you make your artwork big. Give your portrait plenty of room.

6. Public Service: If you are feeling generous, donate your portrait to a local art museum, neighborhood library, or family fridge.

You will need:

✔ pencil, markers, crayons, paints, etc.
✔ blank paper
✔ magnifying lens

What to Do:

1. Walk Your Eyes: As you view the snail through a magnifying lens, pretend your eyes are two tiny ants on a snail-exploring expedition. Allow them to wander over every nook and cranny of the snail's body—up the shell, over the head, everywhere.

Do you wonder about snails? Some kids in El Portal and Claremont did. Here are some of their questions.

How can you make a snail come out?

How fast can they go? How far do they go? Can they swim?

How big do they get? How heavy?

Why don't they have legs or arms?

What do they eat? How do they know where to get food? How come their mouth is on the bottom?

Why do they come out in the rain?

How long have snails been around?

Why are they attracted to objects? Do they know up from down?

Do they have tongues? Ears? Teeth? Bones? Noses? Hair? Nerves?

Do their shells protect them?

Why do snails have antennae? Why do they have four? Why are their eyes on their antennae? Why do their eyes go in and out?

Where is their brain?

How can you tell if they are a boy or a girl?

Why are they slimy? Why do they move slow? How do they crawl?

Why do they leave a gooey trail? What makes them stick to walls?

How many legs do they have?

Why are their shells spiral? How do they get their shell? What colors do they come in?

If their shells break, do they die? Are babies born in their shells?

Are you ready for a potentially wild and crazy challenge? If you raised your hand, all you have to do to get started is focus on a slimy question. Is there something you really wonder about snails? Yes? Well, take that question and follow it. The tips below may help you stay hot on the trail.

Follow That Question

—**Experiment:** Experimentation is one road to discovery. Check out the experiments starting on page 34 to get some ideas of how other people pursued their questions about snails. Could you design an experiment to explore your question?

—**Scrutinize:** Do you think you could answer your question if you did a little more observation? For example, if your question was "Do they have eyes?" do you think you might be able to find the answer if you examined a snail closely through a magnifying lens?

—**Find an Expert:** Do you know any people who know a lot about bugs and other little creatures? Do you think they might be able to answer your question?

—**Research:** Other snailologists may have pondered your question in the past and discovered an answer. Perhaps you could check out some books. In fact, a great book to refer to is this one. Turn the page and search through the next section. If that doesn't work, come back to this page and read on.

Look closely at this critter and see if you can locate eyes, a nose, arms, legs, tentacles, or teeth.

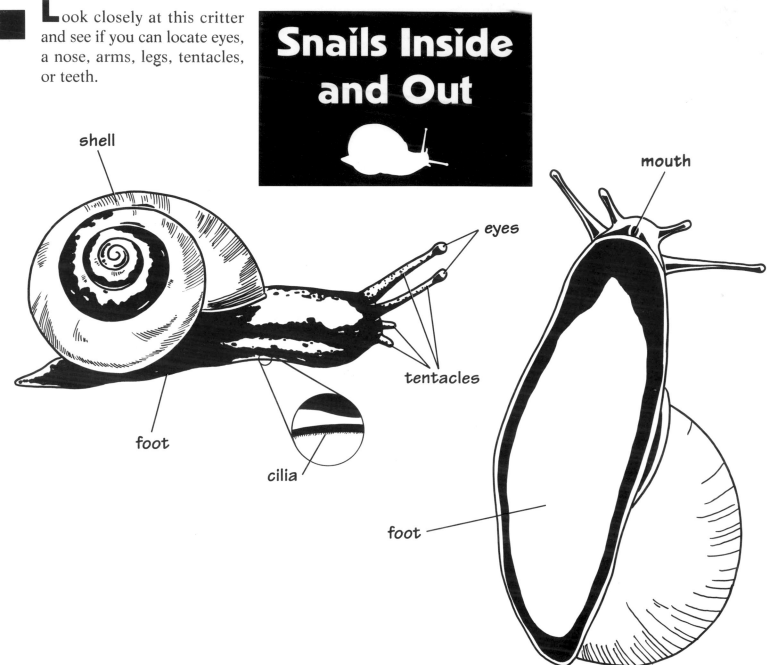

Snails Inside and Out

shell

foot

cilia

eyes

tentacles

mouth

foot

Now peek inside! What can you find? A heart, lungs, or stomach?

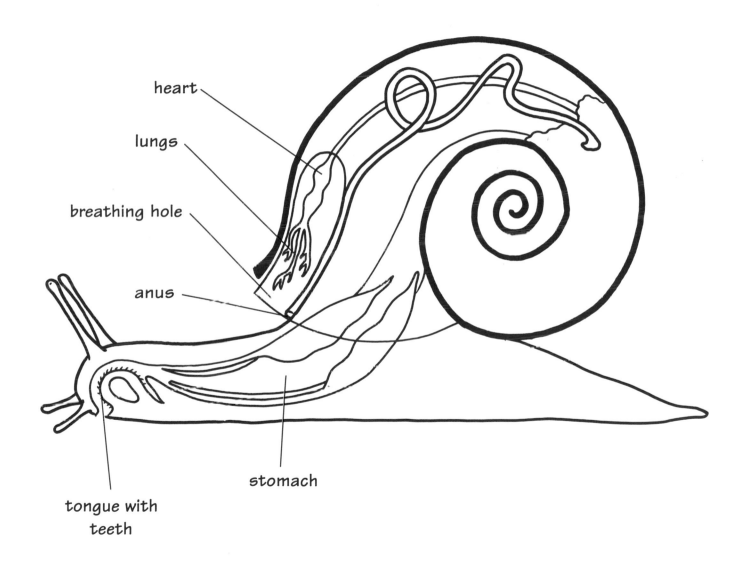

heart

lungs

breathing hole

anus

stomach

tongue with teeth

Mollusks

A mollusk is a soft-bodied creature that has a well-developed head (often with tentacles) and a large, muscular foot. On its top side, it has a **mantle** that grows a shell. The shell can be under the skin like a slug's, in two

Snails and Their Relatives

halves like a clam's, or coiled like a snail's. It's hard to believe, but all the animals below have these same features in common. Mollusks are divided into eight groups, called classes. You may be familiar with the animals in three of the largest classes, which are listed below.

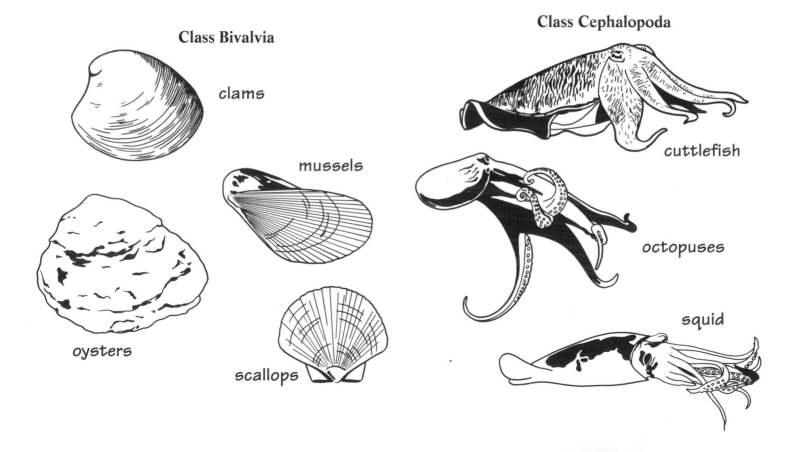

Class Bivalvia

clams

mussels

oysters

scallops

Class Cephalopoda

cuttlefish

octopuses

squid

Class Gastropoda

snails

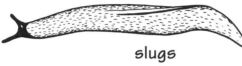

slugs

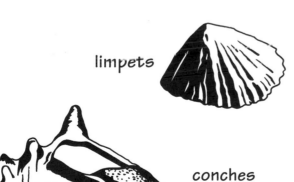

sea slugs

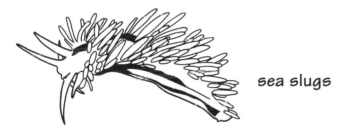

limpets

conches

There are so many kinds of gastropods (over 70,000 species) that scientists have divided them into smaller groups called subclasses!

Subclass Prosobranchia

snails with gills

limpets

conches

Subclass Heterobranchia

sea slugs

snails and slugs (lunged gastropods)

Each subclass is then divided into families. The family Stylomattophora (which means "carriers of drab-colored pointed stakes") is one of the largest families of land snails. It includes common garden snails, such as *Helix aspersa*. (*Helix* means "spiral," and *aspersa* means "scattered.")

What is the strongest animal on Earth?

The snail, because it carries its home on its back.

Carrying your home on your back could be a burden, but it has some advantages too. For one thing, a shell offers protection from **predators**—animals that kill and eat other animals. Have you noticed how a snail goes back into its shell when it is being pestered? Think about it. Wouldn't it be nice at certain times to have your own shell to crawl into?

Consider the shape of the shell you might wear, and then think about the shape of a snail's home. As you crawled along on your belly, what shape would suit you best? A cube, a pyramid, a cylinder, a sphere, or some other shape? Since a pyramid has a wide base and a narrow top, it would rest easily without becoming top-heavy. Since a spiral can be added to at the base, more room could be added as you grew. Since the opening of a coiled shell can be narrow, it makes defense easier. No wonder the spiral pyramid shape is the preferred shell type for land snails throughout the world!

A coiled shell is great if you can fit inside it. To manage this feat, snails have twisted and turned so much that most everything is in a different place from what you would expect. A snail's **genital pore,** the hole through which it releases eggs,

Back Home

is on its head! Meanwhile, its head is on its foot and its teeth are on its tongue. Weirdest of all, its anus, from which it releases **feces,** is next to its breathing hole. Breathing in feces (that's a scientific name for poop) could be a real problem for snails. Fortunately for them, their feces are wrapped in a clear, bag-like **membrane**. To keep the breathing hole clean, snails release feces only when they are exhaling. In this way, they blow feces away from their airholes.

Place your snail in a clear plastic container. Look underneath. Can you see the breathing hole? If you watch for a while, you might notice it breathing or discover exactly where it releases its wastes.

Escargot Anyone?

Despite the protective features of its shell, many a snail ends up as another creature's meal. Young land snails, whose shells are still thin, become **prey** for shrews, rats, and field mice. Birds crack snail shells by hammering them against hard surfaces. Adult snails may be munched by predators such as crows, badgers, foxes, or moles. In some parts of the world, snails are even gnawed by other snails who need a diet of meat.

As people have spread around the world, so have snails. Snail eggs are often accidentally imported with crops from other lands, and the snails that hatch soon establish themselves as official garden pests, eating large numbers of plants. Many of the garden snails we are familiar with are actually from Europe and other continents. The giant African snail, which grows to a length of more than 5 inches, has spread from East Africa to Asia, Australia, and Pacific islands such as Hawaii. Its size and eating habits make it a major pest, and there is a worldwide effort to stop its spread. Despite these efforts, giant African snails made it to the mainland United States in the 1960s, when a boy from Hawaii smuggled some to his grandma in Florida as a gift. After he went home, his grandma released her unwanted pets in the backyard. Within a few years, the giant snails had moved into not only her neighborhood, but neighboring towns.

Although the giant African snail has also invaded Taiwan, it has never been a pest there. Smart Taiwanese businesspeople realized the value of the snails' meat and began exporting snails to France, where people chomp over 45,000 tons a year. *Escargot,* as snail meat is called in France, is a delicacy, and the French can never get enough. One person's pest can be another's treat!

A garden salad is the diet of most land snails, and each snail has just the right equipment for finding and devouring the local leaves. Atop each snail's head, you may have noticed two sets of tentacles. Like the retractable radio antennae on fancy cars, snail tentacles can be pulled back into the head when the snail feels threatened. The upper pair of tentacles has a pair of eyeballs at the tip that can sense light, but would fail most sight tests. These eyes, along with light sensors on the lips, foot, and mantle, enable a snail to seek out moist, dark places where a snail is protected from the blistering sun and hidden from dangerous predators.

Look with Your Lips, Bite with Your Tongue

As a snail glides in the shadows, it uses the other tentacles to feel its way, like a blind person tapping with a cane. Scent detectors on the upper tentacles alert the snail to chemicals given off by food and to the scent of animals that might eat them. Once they locate the local salad bar, snails set their tongues to work.

Each snail tongue is carpeted with rows of tiny sharp teeth. This toothy tongue is called a **radula** (RAH-juh-luh). As a snail rubs a leaf, it scrapes off small bits. Though scraping off a meal with tiny teeth may seem like a slow way to eat, many an irate gardener will tell you that a herd of hungry snails can surely leave its mark.

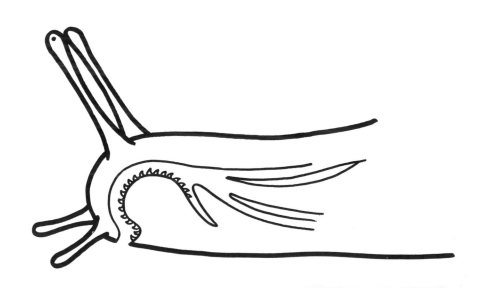

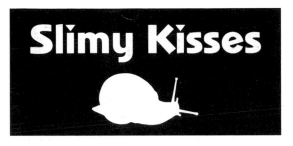

Slimy Kisses

Sometimes a rainy night is all that's needed to send a snail off in search of a mate. With tentacles delicately probing, it investigates the moist shadows for potential partners. Unlike most other animals, it doesn't need to find a mate of the opposite sex. All land snails have both male and female organs. All are capable of being both mother and father.

When a boy/girl snail meets another boy/girl snail, the courtship sometimes begins with a soft brush of the tentacles and a slimy kiss. Soon they may rise up like seals and press their feet together. As they continue to kiss and touch, their heads twist, stretch, and swell. Suddenly one snail may retreat toward its shell, shot by its partner with a small tooth-like dart. Ouch! Can this be called love? Snailologists aren't sure what to call it, but some wonder if shooting the so-called love dart is a test to see if both snails are serious about mating.

If a darted snail comes back out of its shell, it's time indeed for serious action. With feet still pressed together, both snails twist 90 degrees (that's how much you can twist your neck to one side) and fertilize each other's eggs. This process of mixing sperm with eggs may take hours. It is followed by an even longer period of rest.

About a week and a half later, each mother/father seeks out a permanently moist patch under rocks, bark, or leaves, or in the soil. There, the snail buries about 4 dozen grade A snail eggs (one snail in Africa lays eggs the size of real chicken eggs, but most snail eggs are the size of pinheads). By the time the eggs hatch, anywhere from a week to 6 months later, Mom/Dad is long gone. The exception is one species in the South Pacific that hatches eggs inside its shell.

At 2 years of age, when most humans are still wearing diapers, young snails are ready to have babies of their own. Though most snails don't live past 3 to 4 years, a few have been known to reach the ancient age of 7 or 8. It may seem a short life indeed, but it's long enough for the average snail to leave behind more than 500 eggs!

While cheetahs are renowned for running and falcons are famous for flying, snails are recognized for creeping. The word *snail* arose from the Old German root *snahhan,* which means "to creep."

Creepers

Watch a snail as it cruises smoothly over any surface. Have you ever seen anything quite so creepy? Try it yourself. Can you slide across the floor as smoothly? When we try to creep, our movements are jerky, and our clothes snag. Imagine having one large foot and picture yourself sliding along on a bed of jelly.

A close-up peek at a cruising snail's foot with a hand lens may reveal the secret of its smooth moves. For better viewing, place your snail in a clear plastic food container and watch it from below. If you look very carefully, you may be able to see the foot muscles moving in waves. Starting at the front, these waves ripple along the bottom of the foot all the way to the tail end. Like a swimmer doing the backstroke, these backward waves actually move the snail forward. To make this sliding movement smoother, snails release slime from a special mucus gland near the head.

Some species of snails even gallop. Though slower by far than a horse's gallop, this is high-speed travel for a snail. When it gallops, a snail arches the front end of its foot forward while the tail half continues to slide ahead with backward waves.

As you've no doubt noticed, snails are great climbers. Snail slime is sticky as well as slippery and provides them with their amazing grip. Do you wonder, however, how an animal that walks on glue is able to attach itself when it's at rest and detach itself when it's on the move? If this makes you think of suction cups, you're on the right track. The slime is stickiest when pressure is applied, so slime + suction = sticking.

Sublime Slime

Besides being the perfect ooze for a cruise, slime helps snails absorb moisture. When snails are exposed to dry conditions, they are in danger of dying from **dehydration.** By moving to moist or wet areas, they can fill up on water by "drinking" it through their skin. The mucus that coats a snail's skin is like a filter that allows water to pass in.

Snails and slugs sometimes use mucus to defend themselves by gumming up potential predators. Some slugs can even make a slimy rope to lower themselves from trees. Even though we can't do all these nifty things, we do possess slime that is remarkably similar to that of a gastropod.

Does snail slime remind you of the slimy mucus found in your nose and mouth? It not only feels similar, it serves the same purpose. The slimy coatings in our mouth and nose filter out dust and keep in moisture. Though it may not be beautiful, slime is indecd sublime.

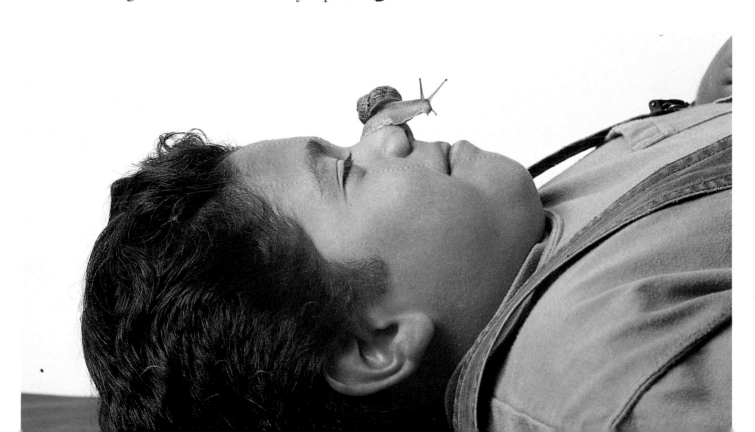

The questions of kid scientists at Valle Vista School in Claremont and my local elementary school in El Portal led to some entertaining and instructive experiments.

Four Short Experiments

Do Snails Like Water?

Allison noticed that when her snail was placed in the water, it retreated into its shell. "It doesn't like water," she commented. Do all land snails react this way when they are placed in water?

How Can You Make a Snail Come Out?

Have you met any snails that prefer just to hang out inside their shells? When Lionel and Mac did, they wondered if they could get the snail to come out. Did the snails need water? The boys placed a snail, still tucked inside its shell, on a wet towel, and waited. After 3 minutes of no action, they moved the snail to a small puddle on the table. Slowly it poked its head out and was soon on the move. Do you think this would work for every snail? How would you know for sure?

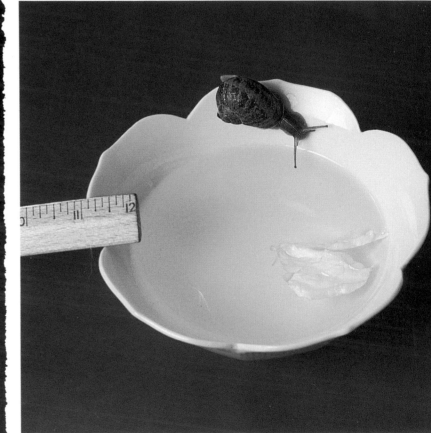

Aaron's snail climbed a ruler to the lip of a bowl of water. He wondered if the snail would swim over to the scrap of lettuce that he placed in the water. What do you think it did? The snail crawled around the rim of the bowl, but after 5 minutes, it still had not taken a dip. What do you think about these different reactions to water? Perhaps snails like just the right amount of moisture, not too much and not too little.

Will Snails Go Up Anything?

Mandy set blocks all over her desk and watched in amazement as her snail climbed over every block that was in its way. "It climbs every block it comes to," she exclaimed. Jeremy observed that his snail continued climbing up a ruler even when he turned the ruler upside down.

Do Snails Prefer Dark Places?

Chris set two containers, one black and one clear, on their sides. After placing his snail between the containers, it cruised into the black one. When he repeated the test, the snail did the same thing. Do you think it would go into the black container every time? Can you think of other ways to determine if snails do indeed like dark places?

Can a Land Snail Swim?

Though some snails live in water, Maria and Kim wondered if a land snail could swim. The test was simple enough. Two different snails were observed in two separate tests. During each test, they were dropped into a clear plastic cup of water.

All the snails stayed afloat when placed in the water. The girls wondered if their shells kept them afloat. Each snail was removed after 4 minutes so they wouldn't be harmed. Below is the girls' record of the snails' actions.

Trial 1

Snail #1: went into its shell after a minute and a half, but came out later.

Snail #2: seemed to want to go into its shell, but didn't go all the way. After a while, it stuck its eyes out.

Trial 2

Snail #1: It looks confused. It appears to want to go into its shell, but doesn't. It just stays at the side of the cup popping its eyes.

Snail #2: Popped its eyes too!

All the snails survived and went back to crawling about on the girls' desktops.

What Can a Snail Climb?

After snailologists from both El Portal and Claremont noticed that snails could climb things, they wondered what snails could climb. Josh discovered that his snail could hang upside down from a lens. Krystale watched her snail walk around the rim of her magnifying lens. Giselle predicted that her snail would lose its grip when it reached the edge of her desk. It did indeed fall, as did several others at nearby desks. Luckily the snails weren't hurt as they dropped onto the carpeted floor.

GJ placed a snail at the bottom of a rope hung from the ceiling. It slowly spiraled up and had reached a height of 43 centimeters by the time the bell rang for recess. James and Logan watched both a small snail and a large snail creep up a 22-inch high sheet of plexiglass. In most of the trials, the snails reached the top in less than 7 minutes, which is faster than some other kids' snails traveled on a flat surface (see next page)!

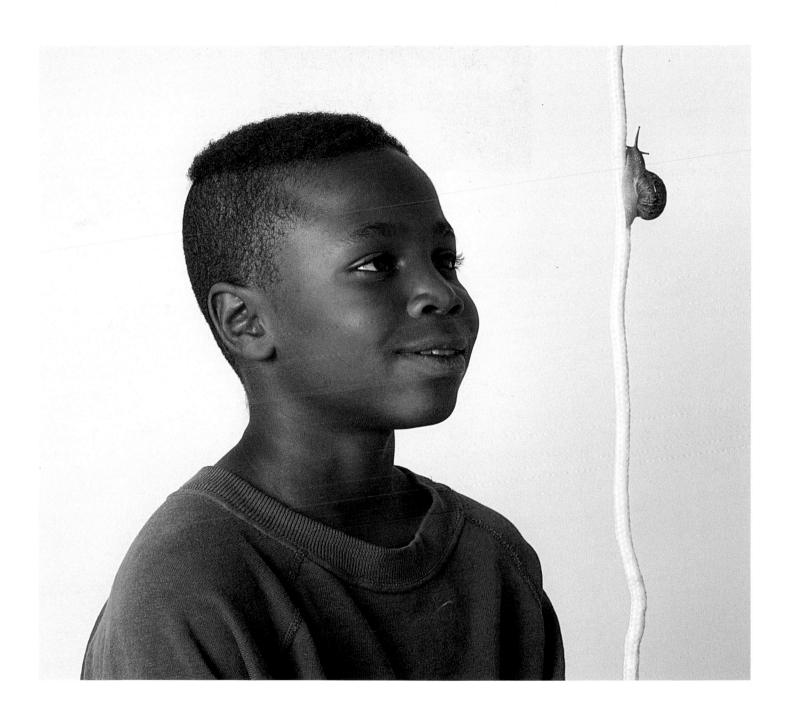

How Fast Does a Snail Travel?

Do you wonder if this is a test of the snail's reputation as a slowpoke? Aaron, Jacob, Caitlin, and Jessica all got out their rulers and watches, and this is what they discovered.

Aaron's snail covered 6½ inches in each 1-minute trial! Jacob's snail cruised 5½ inches in 1 minute. The snails that Caitlin and Jessica watched were considerably faster. Here are the times it took their snails to cruise 1 foot.

Snail #1: 2 minutes
Snail #1: 3 minutes, 21 seconds
Snail #2: 2 minutes, 55 seconds
Snail #2: 2 minutes, 45 seconds

It would take Aaron's snail over 9 days to travel a mile at the same rate at which it moved in his experiment. Jessica and Caitlin's speediest snail would make it in a mere 7⅓ days. Do you have ideas about why some snails were slower? How fast do your slimy friends move?

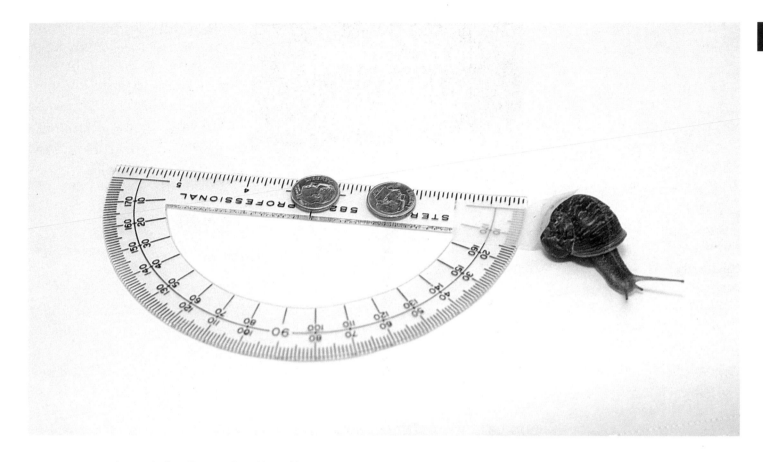

How Much Weight Can a Snail Pull?

Tyler and Jacob noticed that their snails were constant movers, and they wondered if they would still wander with a sled in tow. After the boys discovered that a plastic protractor made a smooth-riding sled, they attached it to a string and taped the string to a snail. Without even pausing, the snail took off, dragging the 2-gram sled. As it moved, the boys gradually added more weight, 2 grams at a time. At 52 grams, the snail was still pulling the sled, but the boys stopped the test because they were concerned about hurting the snail.

With the snail weighing in at 4 grams, the boys calculated that the snail could pull 13 times its own weight. How many times your weight can you pull?

Do your parents ever have difficulty waking you up in time for school? What tactics do they use to get you on the move? Do they try to awaken you, like Sleeping Beauty, with a kiss?

Snails can also be deep sleepers. Perhaps you have already found snails that refuse to wake up. If you look closely at these sluggardly creatures, you may notice that the openings of their shells are sealed shut with dried, booger-like mucus. Like magic window blinds, these **epiphragms** (EH-puh-framz; Latin for "barriers") let in air without letting out much moisture. Thus, during periods of extreme cold, dryness, or food shortage, a snail can remain comfortably moist until better times arrive. Weeks and even months can pass before a snail finally pushes aside the epiphragm with its muscular foot and seeks a meal.

A tap on the shoulder, a blaring alarm, or kiss might wake you, but what awakens a **dormant,** or resting, snail? C. F. Herreid and M. A. Rokitka, a couple of biologists from Buffalo, New York, set up a series of experiments to explore snail alarms.

Snails are more active during periods of heavy dew or rain. Does moist air wake snails from slumber? To find out, Herreid and Rokitka placed groups of 48 snails in dormitories with different relative humidities. Humid air contains large amounts of water vapor, and therefore has a high relative humidity, while dry air has a low one. In chambers where the RH (relative humidity) was less than 58 percent, most of the snails kept snoozing; in chambers with 75 percent or more RH, the snails arose. The higher the RH, the greater the number of snails that woke up. Though moistening the air worked the first time, it failed to awaken most of the snails after their next nap.

Not many snails are seen out and about on scorching hot summer days. Does cool air rouse snails from naps? By exposing dormant snails to air temperatures between 5° centigrade (41° Fahrenheit) and 33° C (91° F), Herreid and Rokitka found out that more woke up at lower temperatures. They also discovered that snails were more likely to arise after long periods of darkness and that hot or cold baths cause them to wake up instantly.

Together, darkness, moist air, and low temperatures are the best wake-up call for snails—better than a radio alarm, a little sister, or the smell of fresh waffles. Many creatures must move or die when their living conditions change. Luckily for snails, they can just hide out in their shells until conditions around them are just right for their survival.

Can you remember special scents? Sniff deeply and imagine the scrumptious smell of your last birthday cake or a favorite fruit that you haven't had for months.

What about a snail? Can it remember its favorite foods? Roger Croll and Ronald Chase, two Canadian snailologists, knew from the work of other scientists that snails can remember adverse stimuli (things that they don't like) for up to 7 weeks. Croll and Chase wondered if snail memory was different when it came to food.

For their experiment, they used the giant African snail, *Achatina fulica*. One group of six adult snails were fed nothing but shredded carrots for 86 days, while another crew of six dined solely on grated cucumber. Both groups were then not fed for 9 days before being tested for food preference in a special Y-shaped odor chamber. Each snail was released in the straight part of the chamber as two streams of air, one smelling of carrots and the other of cucumber, flowed down each arm.

During each 2-day experiment period, each snail was tested four times. After the sessions, the snails were fed lettuce for 4 days, put on a water-only diet for 9 days, and tested again. This pattern was repeated for 4 months.

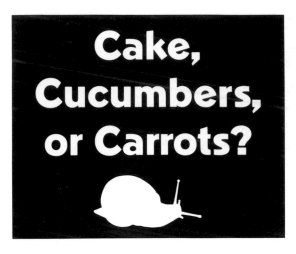

Cake, Cucumbers, or Carrots?

In all of the tests, from beginning to end, the snails went toward the odor of the food they had been fed. Croll and Chase had proved that snails could remember for up to 4 months! Unfortunately, since the tests were not continued, we don't know if snails can remember for even longer periods. Perhaps their memories last for years.

What do you think happened when snails who had not been fed either carrots or cucumbers were tested in the odor chamber? As you might have guessed, these snails had no clear preference for either food.

A snail wandering about in the wild has many plants to munch on. Of course, some may taste yucky, or be poisonous or not nutritious enough. By remembering the scent of delicious, nutritious foods, a snail can stick with the tried and true.

Bad Air and Good Snails

Though hordes of gardeners have tried for centuries to rid gardens of leaf-munching snails, it may be air pollution that finally does them and their important wild relatives in.

The moist beech forests of Scandinavia were once rich with snails. The forests fed the snails leaves, and the snails left behind tons of snail manure, which fertilized the forest soil. These forests were once healthy, but during the last 40 years, as the air in Northern Europe has become more and more polluted, the trees have been dying. At the same time, the number of snails has declined.

Heavy pollution from cars and factories can create acid rain. This rain contains acids that are created when certain gases are mixed with water vapor. Upon hitting the ground, this rain dissolves **calcium** in the soil (just as vinegar, an acid, dissolves baking soda). Since snails need calcium for their shells, it is difficult for them to survive where soil calcium is disappearing.

Ulf Gardenfors, a Swedish scientist, wondered what would happen to snail populations if calcium was added to the forest soil. After observing the snail population in twelve sections of forest, Ulf sprinkled nine plots with lime (a calcium-rich powder made from limestone).

Ulf's survey, 5 years later, showed some remarkable results. In the limed plots, not only were snail populations higher, but more species of snails were present. More lime means more snails, which could be welcome news for sensitive snails. In the short run, perhaps lime can be used to save snails from pollution; in the long run, perhaps we can save even more than snails by working to keep our air a bit cleaner.

GLUB.... GLUB... GLUB...

MILK WITH ADDED CALCIUM

Can you believe that you read a whole book about snails and still have questions that haven't been answered? Maybe this book is too slim, or perhaps it doesn't matter what size it is because your questions can't be answered by any book. Maybe no one has ever tried to answer them before. To a scientist, an easily answered question is like a piece of stale bread, while a

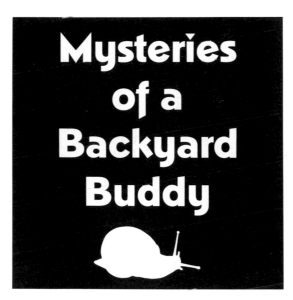

difficult question is worth slobbering over. Ponder your delicious questions once more and consider the outrageous investigations they can lead you into. Lick your lips and follow your nose.

Here are some killer questions that kids from Claremont and El Portal may still be trying to answer at this very moment.

How smart are snails?

How do snails communicate?

Why do they have goosebumps?

Do they have feelings?

Do their shells feel heavy to them?

Do they hate salt?

Why don't they have legs?

Why do they crawl up on each other?

What leftover questions do you have?

Glossary

calcium: a mineral that many animals, including snails, need for the development of their skeletons or shells

dehydration: the condition of not having enough water or moisture

dormant: asleep or inactive

epiphragm: a layer of mucus that a snail produces and uses to seal its shell shut, protecting itself from cold, dryness, or food shortages

feces: an animal's solid wastes

gastropods: a group of mollusks that includes snails and slugs. Gastropods have their mouths on their feet.

genital pore: an opening through which some animals, including snails, release eggs

gills: structures that some animals, including some types of snails, use for breathing

mantle: a structure on a snail's body that produces the snail's shell

membrane: a thin layer of tissue

mollusks: a group of animals with soft bodies and, usually, hard shells

predators: animals that kill and eat other animals

prey: animals that are killed and eaten by other animals

radula: a tongue-like structure that is covered with teeth

species: A group of animals with common traits, especially their ability to produce young

tentacles: arm-like structures on a snail's head that are used for sensing

Index

About the Author

For the last twenty years, Michael Elsohn Ross has taught visitors to Yosemite National Park about the park's wildlife and geology. Mr. Ross, his wife, Lisa (a nurse who served nine seasons as a ranger-naturalist), and their son, Nick, have led other families on wilderness expeditions from the time Nick learned to crawl. Mr. Ross studied conservation of natural resources at the University of California/Berkeley, with a minor in entomology (the study of insects). He spent one summer at Berkeley raising thousands of red-humped caterpillars and parasitic wasps for experiments.

Mr. Ross makes his home on a bluff above the wild and scenic Merced River, at the entrance to Yosemite. His backyard garden is a haven for rolypolies, crickets, snails, slugs, worms, and a myriad of other intriguing critters.

NOV 1999

PURCHASED AT PUBLIC SALE
SURPLUS MATERIALS FROM THE SLCLS